THE POWER OF CONSISTENCY

Dr. Syed Kazim

Copyright © 2020 Dr. Syed Kazim
All rights reserved.
ISBN: 9798690159313

CONTENTS

I. Religion

1	God wants Consistency	2
2	World's Quickest Revolution	4
3	The Ultimate Schedule	14
4	Two Days Equal = Loser	17
5	Taking Bath Five Times a Day	19
6	Magic of Charity	21
7	950 Years	23

II. People

1	One Handed Gold Medalist	27
2	One Armed Boy	30
3	Declared Clinically Dead	32
4	The $1,00,000 Painting	36
5	Goal Post is Small	38
6	Reading Leading	40
7	4 AM	42
8	Bowl Out at T20 World Cup	44
9	23 Golds	47
10	Squeeze – Shape – Cut – Fry	49
11	One Percent	51
12	13 Virtues and 52 Weeks	53
13	Block and Punch	57
14	Super 30	59

15	Computer Boy	62
16	Piston Ring to Motorcycle	64
17	The Mountain Man	67
18	What is Your Job?	70
19	3 Kilometer in 30 Years	72
20	It Will Never Fail You	74

III. Stories, Events and Research

1	Hare and Tortoise	79
2	Cracked Pot	81
3	Fighting Cancer	83
4	Water Torture	85
5	Sharpen Your Saw	87

IV. Concepts

1	5 Dimensions of Improvement	90
2	Kaizen	94
3	Jack of All, Master of One	98
4	Conscious Competence	101
5	Chinese Bamboo Tree	104
6	Life Long Learner	106
7	10,000 Hours	108

V. Why and How?

1	Brain and Consistency	112
2	Secret of Achieving Mastery	115

THE POWER OF CONSISTENCY

THE POWER OF CONSISTENCY

I
Religion

1.1

God Loves Consistency

Ayesha reported, the Messenger of God said, "Follow the right course, seek nearness to God, and give glad tidings. Verily, none of you will enter Paradise by his deeds alone. They said, "Not even you, O Messenger of God?" The Prophet said, "Not even me, unless God grants me his mercy. Know that the most beloved deed to God is that which is done regularly, even if it is small" (Bukhari).

In another narration, Ayesha reported, the Prophet Muhammad entered while I was with another woman. The Prophet asked, "Who is this?" I said, "She is a woman who never sleeps because she is always praying". The Prophet said, "You must only perform deeds you are capable of doing. By God, God will not withhold from you until you give up. The most beloved religious deeds to God are those performed consistently" (Bukhari).

This clearly indicates that it is the consistency of our deeds that counts more than anything else. Even if they are few, we should perform it consistently. God loves people doing deeds consistently even if they are small and easy. Islam has given high importance to consistency in various aspects of one's life. The first is the five daily prayers that have to be performed consistently without fail. The next is fasting consistently in the month of Ramadan for 29 or 30 days, every year.

In order to create a positive impact, we need to strive to be consistent in every aspect of our lives. We need to be consistent in all acts of worship, if we become consistent in all acts of worship, then we would become consistent in all other aspects of our life. The acts of worship would act as training for an individual to be consistent in all other aspects of his life. Whatever activity we do, we need to strive for excellence and excellence can only be achieved through consistency.

1.2

World's Quickest Revolution

Prophet Muhammad attained Prophethood at the age of 40. From that day he did not rest even for a day. He consistently worked toward accomplishing the mission which was given to him by God. That is the reason why the Prophet was able to create a complete revolution over a period of less than 23 years. The revolution created by Prophet is considered to be the world's quickest revolution, took less than 23 years to accomplish, 1400 years back. As soon as Prophet attained Prophethood, he started his work. Details are mentioned as follows:

Year 1 - 3 (610 – 612)
- The first three years, the Prophet began preaching in secret.
- He first went to the 4 closest people in his life and conveyed the message of Islam. They were his wife Khadijah, friend Abu Bakar, cousin Ali ibn Abu Talib, and slave Zayd ibn Harithah, all of them accepted Islam.

- Then Prophet took Dar Al-Arqam, the house of Al-Arqam ibn Abul-Arqam Al-Makhzumi on As-Safa as their office and a temporary center form movement and meetings. The center was also used to give the teachings of the Qur'an to the people who accepted Islam. During this period around 40 people accepted Islam.

Year 4 (613)

- The Prophet went on to make a public announcement of Prophethood.
- Mild oppression of new Muslims (Especially the slaves) started by the Quraish of Mecca by adopting various cheap means and the Prophet tried his best to counter their oppression.
- The Quraish pressurized Abu Talib, the uncle of Prophet to stop his call toward one God, but the Prophet did not agree to it and said at any cost he would abandon his call until God will make him victorious.

Year 5 (614)

- The Quraish started atrocities against the Prophet and his family and the Prophet did his best to face them.
- Quraish of Mecca continued torturing weak Muslims which Prophet and other new Muslims were trying their best to rescue the new converts.

Year 6 (615)

- The Quraish of Mecca continued torturing the Muslims through various methods and the Prophet was busy coming up with solutions to overcome the oppression which they were facing.
- As the oppression became unbearable, and reached its peak, then Prophet decided and sent a few companions to Abyssinia (Ethiopia).

Year 7 – 10 (616 - 619)

- When the oppression continued the Prophet decided to send a second group of people to Abyssinia.
- As the Quraish were having various problems with the Prophet, they came to him to negotiate to give-up his call, but the Prophet did not agree to their offer and continues propagating Islam in Mecca.
- The Quraish started a social and economic boycott to the clan of the Prophet, so the Prophet was busy coming up with activities to counter them.
- The Prophet married Sawdah.

Year 11 (620)

- The Prophet visited Taif, a place which was 60 km from Mecca, to invite people to Islam.
- The Prophet began introducing and inviting individuals and tribes to Islam.
- The Prophet met a group of Prophet from Madina (Yathrib) during the pilgrimage season and conveyed the message of Islam, which resulted in 6 people, accepted Islam.

- The Prophet married Ayesha

Year 12 (621)

- The Prophet also took the journey of Meraj.
- The first Aqabah Pledge with a group of 12 people from Madina and the Prophet.
- The Prophet assigned Musab ibn Umair to go to Madina and teach Islam, who went on to become the first ambassador of Islam.

Year 13 (622)

- The second Aqabah Pledge came into place during the pilgrimage season with over 70 people who had accepted Islam from Madina. The pledge a strong foundation for Prophet to move to Madina.
- The Prophet asked the companions to start emigration to Madina.
- The Prophet makes a plan to leave Mecca and migrates to Madina.
- The Prophet reached Quba, stayed there for 4 days, builds a Masjid, and prayed there.
- After 8 days of the journey, the Prophet reached Madina; the Prophet constructed a mosque and introduced azan.

Year 14 (623) – (1 A.H.)

- Prophet established brotherhood between Muhajireen (Emigrants) and Ansar (Helpers).

- The Madina contract was drawn with the people of Median (Jews and Polytheists) with an objective to provide peace, security, and prosperity to all the people of Madina.
- The Prophet set up an army.
- A marketplace was established in Madina by Prophet.

Year 15 (624) – (2 A.H.)
- Various missions and invasions such as the Saiful-Bahr Mission, Rabigh Mission, Kharrar Mission, Invasion of Al-Abwa/Waddan, Invasion of Buwat, Invasion of Safwan, Invasion of Dhil-Ushairah, and Nakhlah Mission took place.
- Battle of Badar.
- The Prophet laid Siege to the Jews forts.
- Invasion of As-Saweeq and Dhi Amr and Buhran took place.
- The Prophet married Ayesha.
- The Prophet married his daughter Fathima to Ali.
- The Prophet observed Ramadan for the first time.

Year 16 (625) – (3 A.H.)
- Battle of Uhad.
- The Invasion of Hamra'ul-Asad took place.
- The Invasion of Al-Kudr and Bani Qainuqa took place.

Year 17 (626) – (4 A.H.)
- Mission of Abi Salamah.
- Mobilization of Abdullah ibn Unais Ar-Raji and Najd to teach and preach Islam.
- Invasion of Bani An-Nadeer.

- The Second Battle of Badar.
- The Invasion of Dumatul-Jandal.

Year 18 (627) – (5 A.H.)
- Census of Madina was conducted.
- Battle of Trench/Invasion of Al-Ahzab.
- The Invasion of Banu Quraidah.

Year 19 (628) – (6 A.H.)
- Expedition to Al-Ghamr inhabited by Bani Asad, Bani Tha'labah in Dhul-Qassah, Al-Jamum area of Bani Sulaim in Marr Az-Zahran, Al-Eis, Bani Tha'labah at the place Taraf and Wadi Al-Qura.
- The Invasion of Bani Al-Mustaliq.
- Expedition to Bani Kalb in Dumatal-Jandal in Sha'ban, Bani Sa'd ibn Bakr in a place called Fadak, Wadi Al-Qura, and Urainah.
- Prophet along with companions went to Mecca to perform Umrah but let to the Treaty of Hudaybiya.
- The Prophet planned to spread the message of Islam beyond Arabia.

Year 20 (629) – (7 A.H.)
- The Prophet wrote a letter to Abyssinia (Ethiopia), King of Egypt called Muqawqis, Chosroes – Emperor of Persia, Envoy of Caesar – King of Rome, Mundhir ibn Sawa – Governor of Bahrain, Haudhah ibn Ali – Governor of Yamamah, Al-Harith ibn Abi Shimr Al-Ghassani – King of Damascus, King of Oman,

Jaifer and his brother Abd ibn Al-Julandai, inviting them to Islam.

- The Invasion of Ghabah/Dhi Qarad.
- The Conquest to Khaybar.
- The Invasion to Dhat-ur-Riqa.
- The Prophet along with 2000 men performed the Compensatory Umrah.
- The Prophet sends people to habitations of Bani Sulaim and invited them to embrace Islam.
- The Invasion of Fadak and Banu Quda'ah.

Year 21 (630) – (8 A.H.)

- The Invasion of Bani Hawazin.
- Battle of Ma'tah.
- The Mission of Dhatus-Salasil and Khadrah.
- The conquest of Mecca.
- The Prophet dispatched platoons to Nakhlah, Hudhail, Al-Mushallal, and Bani Jadhimah.
- The Battle of Hunayn.
- The Invasion of Ta'if.
- The Prophet performed Umrah.
- Prophet sent a second letter to the Emperor of Byzantium inviting him to Islam.

Year 22 (631) – (9 A.H.)

- Prophet sends a platoon to Bani Tamim, Khath'am tribe in Tabalah and Bani Kilah.
- The Battle of Tabuk.

- The Prophet took a 20-day spiritual retreat in Ramadan and recited the Qur'an twice with Ark Angel Gibreel.
- The Prophet sent Abu Bakar as the deputy to perform Hajj with the companions.

Year 23 (632) – (10 A.H.)

- People started entering into the fold of Islam in huge numbers.
- The Prophet ensured that the state is run as per the principles given in the Qur'an.
- A number of delegations such as Suda, Udhrah, Bali, Thaqif, Hamdan, Bani Fazarah, Najran, Bani Delegation, Bani Air ibn Sa'sa'ah, Tujeeb, and Ta'i came to meet Prophet and discuss various religious, social, and political issues.
- The Prophet went to Hajj.

This is how the Prophet kept himself completely busy during his term as a Prophet. During his entire 23 years, the Prophet kept on preaching Islam and inviting people to worship the one true God. During his 10 years in Madina, the Prophet constantly ensures that the state should be run on the principles given by God, which were mentioned in the Qur'an. The daily schedule of the Prophet will also help us to understand the consistency of the Prophet which has been mentioned in the next chapter of the book.

The revolution which was created by Prophet was a comprehensive one, as it completely moved people from darkness to light.

Before Prophet Muhammad	After Prophet Muhammad
True concept of God was Lost	True concept of God was Restored
Ignorance	Knowledge
Barbarism and Ruthlessness	Kindness and Mercy
Usury and Exploitation	Justice and Fairness
Fear and Terror	Peace and Security
Class and Colour Discrimination	Love and Brotherhood
Children were treated as Slaves	Children were treated with Respect
Girls were Killed	Girls were Loved and Cared
Strongest Man would take over the Property	Property was Rightly Distributed
People became Leaders based on their Influence	People became Leaders in a Democratic Manner
Sexual Slavery, Nudity and Persecution of Women	Women were given Status and Rights

Michael H. Hart, in his book 'The 100: A Ranking of the Most Influential Persons in History' ranked Prophet Muhammad at the number 1 position and said, "My choice of Muhammad to lead the list of the world's most influential persons may surprise some readers and may be questioned by others, but he was the only man in history who was supremely successful on both the religious and secular levels". Prophet Muhammad was able to accomplish the mission in a span of 23 years on both the religious and secular front only because of his consistent effort. Thus, if one wants to contribute significantly and create a difference, then consistency is the way forward.

1.3

The Ultimate Schedule

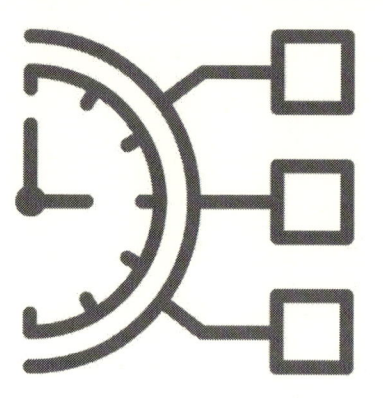

Umm Salamah reported the most beloved deed to the Messenger of God is what is done consistently even if it is small. (Musnad Aḥmad). Alqamah reported, I asked Ayesha, "O mother of the believers, how were the deeds of the Messenger of God? Did he designate anything for certain days?" Ayesha said, "No. The Messenger of God would perform deeds regularly, and who among you are capable of doing as he did? (Bukhari).

Abu Huraira reported, the Messenger of God said, "Take up good deeds only as much as you are able, for the best deeds are those done regularly even if they are few" (Ibn Majah). Ayesha said, "When the household of Prophet Muhammad committed to an act of worship, they would do it consistently" (Muslim).

Prophet effectively channelized his time from Tahajjud (Night Prayer) to Isha. He would get up for Tahajjud and after that; he would take a brief nap and then head for Fajar (Early Morning) prayer. After the obligatory prayer, he would perform the adhkar (Praising God) and address the companions till sunrise. After sunrise, the Prophet Muhammad would visit his house and then come back to the Mosque. There he would address the companions on various issues, answer their questions, meet people who had come to meet him and receive delegations. He would greet them, seek their news, and see how he could help them.

Prophet Muhammad would also visit his relatives and companions, or those not feeling well. He would walk through the market, greeting passers-by. He would greet children on his way, and if a person stopped him, he would stop and listen to them and see how he could help them. The women of Madinah would come and visit the Prophet Muhammad and ask questions about their religion. They would be embarrassed to ask in a crowded masjid. He would help his family, serving them, repairing his shoes and clothes, milking sheep, and helping with daily chores.

After Zohar (Afternoon) prayer, he would go the minbar (pulpit) and address the companions. He could return home and pray two rakah (cycle) of Zohar, and then he'd go out with his companions to look after the needs of the city or he'd stay in the Mosque till Asar (Evening) prayer. Asar prayer, he would visit his wives and settle in a wife's house.

After Maghrib (Late Evening) prayer, he would sometimes invite companions to dinner. The meal never went by without a pleasing talk or teaching of manners. After performing Isha prayer, he would go back to his house. He would spend time with his family, talking, smiling, and laughing with them. Sometimes, he would go to his close companions' houses and spend time with them, especially his close friends Abu Bakar and Umar, and then go to sleep. All this was possible every single day, as Prophet Muhammad utilized his time in the most effective manner.

During the time of peace, Prophet Muhammad arranged for regular military training of adult Muslim men. Races of horses and camels were organized. Wrestling matches were also held. Training in archery was imparted and prizes were awarded to winners in all events. The army remained in a state of readiness during the time of peace. Its effectiveness was determined by the depth of its faith and the strength of its training. In all these activities, the Prophet Muhammad was consistent, thus, it helped him to create a deep impact on the people around him and the society in which he lived.

1.4

Two Days Equal = Loser

Prophet Muhammad said, "He whose two days are equal, is a loser" (Daiylami). One should always try to have his 'today' better than his 'yesterday'. One should keep increasing in piety and good deeds. One should try to devote more time, energy, and resources with each passing day to win God's pleasure. One should want his inner self to be better 'today' than it was 'yesterday' and his 'tomorrow' to be better than 'today'. One should not want to repeat his mistakes, which he has learned from his experiences, and try to purify his hearts and his intentions to make them better all the time. Thus, his two days will not be equal only when he is consistently working hard and learning or doing something new every day.

If each day we make only one tiny improvement; do one additional act of charity, learn one small thing, reads a few pages of a book, think of how much one would improve over time. A person's competition should be with him because when one gets better, he would gain more of God's pleasure and thus gaining higher and better status in this world and the hereafter.

Every day one should introspect and see what new he has learned or done on that particular day. These daily assessments will help the individual to understand his strengths and weaknesses, and ultimately help him to improve.

In order to be a winner, one should continually strive to improve himself by gaining knowledge, learning a particular skill, etc. A person who is not consistent will not achieve anything significant in his life, and one might end up being a loser. Thus, continuous growth and development are very much necessary for a man, if he wants to achieve something extraordinary in life.

1.5

Taking Bath Five Times a Day

Prophet Muhammad said, "If there was a river at your door and he took a bath in it five times a day, would you notice any dirt on him?". They (Companions) said, "Not a trace of dirt would be left." The Prophet said, "That is the parable of the parable of the five prayers by which God removes sins" (Bukhari and Muslim).

The hadith (saying) uses two techniques of giving examples and questioning to explain the concept. The hadith is an explanation about the benefit of performing five daily prayers, which are mandatory in Islam. The hadith has relating 'taking bath at a river five times a day' to 'performing five prayers on a daily basis'. The result of taking bath five times a day would make the person physically clean without any dirt left on his body, similarly, when a person performs five prayer daily then God would remove and forgive all his sins. This also helps us to learn that performing prayer consistently would help us to get our sins removed and thereby cleanses and purifies the soul of a Muslim.

Consistent prayers do not only get our sins removed but it also helps to abstain from sins as God says, "Recite, (O Muhammad), what has been revealed to you of the Book and establish prayer. Indeed, prayer prohibits immorality and wrongdoing, and the remembrance of God is greater. And God knows that which you do" (Qur'an 29:45). Prayer softens the heart of a Muslim and it naturally prevents you from committing sins because it teaches you to be humble and disciplines your life. Thus, the essence of the consistently praying the five daily prayers in Islam cannot be underestimated. It is an act that would give a person success in the world and in the hereafter.

1.6

Magic of Charity

Abu Huraira narrated from Prophet Muhammad that, once while a man was traveling in the wilderness he heard a voice in a cloud ordering the angel of the cloud to pour its rain on a particular farm. So, the man followed the cloud and saw that it poured its rain on a rocky volcanic plain. All the water gathered in a stream and poured into a farm. The man saw the owner working in that farm and asked him his name. The name was the same one that he had heard from the cloud. The man then related what he had heard and seen, and inquired from the owner of the farm what was special about him that would explain all of this. Given the reason for the inquiry, the owner explained that he would plant his farm and then split the harvest into three equal parts. One part he gave as charity, the second part he kept as food for himself and his family, and the third part he replanted (Muslim).

The hadith basically talks about the benefit which one would get when he indulges in the act of giving consistent charity. The hadith gives the formula to get the help and support of God, through ways, which man cannot expect or imagine.

The man was giving one-third of his earnings as a charity on a consistent basis. This is why God was sending rain especially for him. Giving charity is good, but giving it consistently is even better. It is always better to do small consistent deeds rather than big, infrequent ones. Thus, God was sending provisions to the man (in the form of rain) because of his consistent charity.

1.7
950 years

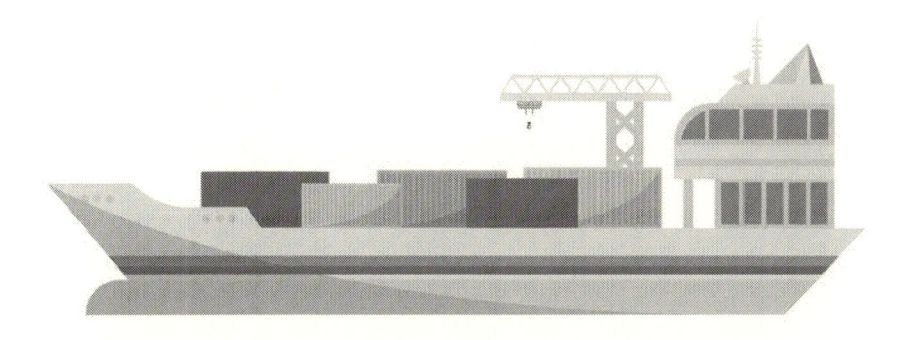

God says, "And We certainly sent Noah to his people, and he remained among them a thousand years minus fifty years, and the flood seized them while they were wrongdoers" (Qur'an 29:14).

From the time Prophet Noah was appointed as a Prophet, till the coming of the flood, he went on making efforts for 950 years for the reformation of his wicked people, and he did not lose heart even though he suffered persecutions for such a long time. The same is the aim of the discourse here. The believers are being told that you have been suffering persecutions and experiencing the stubbornness of your wicked opponents hardly for six years or so. Just imagine the patience and resolution and firmness of Our servant who braved such afflictions and hardships continuously for nine and a half centuries.

It happened that every passing generation admonished the succeeding one not to believe Prophet Noah and to wage war against him. A father used to teach his child about the matter that was between himself and Prophet Noah and counsel him to reject his call when he reached adulthood. Their natural disposition rejected believing and following the truth. Prophet Noah saw that the number of believers was not increasing, while that of the disbelievers was. He was sad for his people, but he never reached the point of despair and kept patience (Ibn Kathir). In spite of such unfavorable situations, Prophet Noah remained consistent and steadfast in his mission. He remained consistent in calling people to believe in the one true God for 950 years.

Another task gives to Prophet Noah was the construction of a ship. God says, "And he constructed the ship, and whenever an assembly of the eminent of his people passed by him, they ridiculed him. He said, "If you ridicule us, then we will ridicule you just as you ridicule" (Qur'an 11:38). When Prophet Noah started constructing the ship on dry land, the opponents ridiculed him. They were not prepared to imagine that a gigantic flood could at all come and in that only the ship of Prophet Noah could be saved. So, they taunted Prophet Noah and the other Muslims who were constructing the ship. By the comment, Prophet Noah was not dejected or disheartened but neglected the comment and continued to be consistent in his task of constructing the ship.

Prophet Noah remained consistent until the last minute, with the task given to him. God says, "And it sailed with them through waves like mountains, and Nuh called to his son who was apart (from them), "O my son, come aboard with us and be not with the disbelievers" (Qur'an 11:42). One of the sons of Prophet Noah was a disbeliever, so he was not on the ship. Prophet Noah called his son in the midst of the storm to come with the believers when he was surrounded with water from all the sides and the distance between him and death was only a few minutes away. Prophet Noah did his best, did not lose his hope, and tried till the last minute so that his son could join him on the ship so that he could be saved.

In the end, all his consistency paid off, Prophet Noah was able to escape the grave flood with around 70 to 80 people who boarded the ship with him. After the flood settled, these were the people who continued to follow and propagate the message of God to the entire mankind.

II
People

2.1

One Handed Gold Medalist

Karoly Takacs was from Hungary and was the best pistol shooter of his country. He was born in the year 1910. By 1936, he was a world-class pistol shooter and was the best pistol shooter of Hungary, as he had won all the national competitions. He was denied a place in the Hungarian shooting team for the 1936 Summer Olympics on the grounds that he was a sergeant, and only commissioned officers were allowed to compete, later the prohibition was lifted. He was such a great shooter that people knew that Karoly is going to win the gold media in the 1940 Olympics.

In 1938, during the army training camp, a faulty grenade exploded in his hand and he lost his hand. At the time point of time, he was 28 years old. He was hospitalized and underwent treatment for one month. He was determined to continue his shooting career and switched to shooting with his left hand. After the treatment, he started his shooting practice consistently for 1 year.

THE POWER OF CONSISTENCY

In the year 1939, he came back when the National championship was being held. Many other pistol shooters met him and appreciated him that even after a severe accident; he has come back to see the sport and to boost their confidence. No one knew that he was consistently training himself to compete with them. All of them were competing with their 'best hand' and he was competing with his 'only hand. Karoly went on to win the Hungarian National Pistol Shooting Championship.

His only aim was the make his hand the best shooting hand in the world and he was successful. He put his complete focus and attention on the 1940 Olympics, as he had only 1 year left and started his practice. Unfortunately, the 1940 Olympic was canceled due to the Second World War. He never gave up, he put his complete focus on the 1944 Olympics, but unfortunately, even the 1944 Olympics were canceled due to Second World War.

He did not lose hope and put his complete focus on the 1948 Olympics. Now he is 38 years old. During this period of 10 years, many young players had come up and competed with them made the task more difficult. He went ahead to participate in the 1948 Olympic, where he had to face the world's best shooters, who were competing with their 'best hand' and he was competing with his 'only hand'. He went on to win a gold medal in the 1948 Olympics.

He went on to beat the favorite, Argentine Carlos Enrique Diaz Saenz Valiente, who was the reigning world champion, who had approached him before the event and had asked him what he was doing there (having heard about his accident). His reply was that he was there to learn and set a world record.

He did not spot here, he went ahead to participate in the 1952 Olympics and again won a gold medal. After the match, Valiente congratulated him again and said "you have learned more than enough now it's time to teach me". His story has given him a place among the 'Olympic Heroes' of the International Olympic Committee.

This win changed the entire history of the Olympic, as no one ever before had won 2 gold medals consecutively in the 25-meter rapid fire pistol shooting competition, both with his left hand. He was also the only third physically disabled athlete to have competed in the Olympic Games, at that time. All this was possible because of his consistent effort and practice, which paid off in the end.

2.2

One Armed Boy

Once, a 10-year-old boy decided to join judo despite the fact that he had lost his left arm in a devastating car accident. His parents were delighted and got him enrolled. The boy began lessons with an old Japanese judo master. The boy was doing well, so he couldn't understand why, after three months of training the master had consistently taught him only one move.

The boy finally asked his master, "Shouldn't I be learning more moves?" The master replied, "This is the only move you know, but this is the only move you'll ever need to know". Not quite understanding, but believing in his master, the boy kept training.

Several months later, the master took the boy to his first tournament. Surprising himself, the boy easily won his first two matches. The third match proved to be more difficult, but after some time, his opponent became impatient and charged; the boy deftly used his one move to win the match. Still amazed by his success, the boy was now in the finals.

This time, his opponent was bigger, stronger, and more experienced. For a while, the boy appeared to be overmatched. Concerned that the boy might get hurt, the referee called a time-out. He was about to stop the match when the master intervened. "No", the master insisted, "Let him continue". Soon after the match resumed, his opponent made a critical mistake, he dropped his guard. Instantly, the boy used his move to pin him. The boy had won the match and the tournament. He was the champion.

On the way home, the boy and the master reviewed every move in each and every match. Then the boy summoned the courage to ask what was really on his mind. "Master, how did I win the tournament with only one move?" The master replied, "You won for two reasons. First, you've almost mastered one of the most difficult throws in all of the judo, which you consistently practiced for the first three months. And second, the only known defense for that move is for your opponent to grab your left arm, which you don't have".

The boy's biggest weakness had become his biggest strength. This was only possible because of his consistent and dedicated effort. Bruce Lee once said, "I am not afraid of the person who kicks in 10,000 different ways, but I am afraid of the person who has practiced one kick 10,000 times because if he kicks me, I will fall down".

2.3
Declared Clinically Dead

Once, a 20-year-old boy by the name of Hal Elrod was driving his new car at 70 mph. He was hit head-on by a drunken driver in a truck traveling 80 mph the wrong way on the highway when he was 20 years old. Metal crumpled; the windshield shattered; and the car was thrown into oncoming traffic, where another car hit the vehicle again. His car was cut in half, and his body was pinned inside by the steering wheel. When rescue workers pulled the car's twisted frame away from his broken body, they literally killed him.

After the horrific car accident, he was declared clinically dead for 6 minutes, as he suffered multiple internal injuries and his heart had stopped beating. Over the next six days, Hal Elrod had seven surgeries to repair 11 broken bones, a shattered spleen, and disconnected nerves. When he woke from his coma he was told by doctors that he would never walk again. When he finally regained consciousness, he couldn't walk, one arm curled back against his chest, his short-term memory was shot, and he had lost the ability to filter his comments for social acceptability. Day by day he improved. Seven weeks after his accident, Elrod left the hospital. Soon he was back at work.

He began shifting toward his next career as a life coach and motivational speaker. He became certified as a life coach, accepted speaking engagements, and began writing a book. Although he wasn't a natural writer, Elrod pushed himself and was consistent, which result in producing the book 'Taking Life Head On! (The Hal Elrod Story): How to Love the Life You Have While You Create the Life of Your Dreams'. It was a huge success and launched his new career.

In the wake of several years of achievement, the global financial crisis slammed Elrod. Tight money dried up his speaking engagements; coaching clients canceled their contracts. Right after buying a house and getting engaged, Elrod lost half his income and found himself $425,000 in debt. He had become deeply depressed and was on a downward spiral that lasted for six months. He finally reached the point that I couldn't get out of bed and he began to contemplate suicide.

He hit bottom twice in his life, once after his horrific automobile accident and again after suffering extreme financial setbacks during the Great Recession. His second incident was the more harrowing experience because there were a lot of people taking care of me after the accident and he had no one when he was facing financial issues during the economic crisis.

With the help of his friend Jon Berghoff, Elrod literally pulled himself out of bed to go running. The benefits of exercise opened Hal Elrod to consider the benefits of an hour-long morning routine. He initially used to hate mornings. With his friend's encouragement, Hal Elrod who had previously hated running began covering long distances. The man was who was declared clinically dead for 6 minutes, who had been cautioned that he might never walk again, completed a 52-hour ultra-marathon.

He rises early in order to have an hour to focus on the day, and he's inspiring others to do the same. He said, "I'm a work in progress, and people know it. I think that's why people relate to me. We're all fighting the same battles."

This inspired him to write 'The Miracle Morning' which went on to become a world bestseller. The book has been translated into 27 languages, has over 2,000 five-star Amazon reviews, and is practiced daily by over 5 lakh people in 70+ countries. In the book, he presents steps for laying a positive foundation for the day. The benefit of the activities which have been mentioned in the book has always been known, but the difference is concentrating them into an efficient program and then taking the time to actually do it.

The book basically talks about 6 activities that would transform life, which have to be done before 8 AM. In his book, Hal Elrod encourages readers to get up an hour earlier than usual every day and perform 6 activities on a consistent basis, so that it becomes a habit. He says that our morning routine affects our levels of success in every single area of our life. Focused, productive, successful mornings generate focused, productive, successful days. In his book, he calls the 6 activities as Life

S.A.V.E.R.S. program, which comprises of 6 activities. S.A.V.E.R.S. stands for Silence, Affirmation, Visualization, Exercise, Reading, and Scribing. He would get up early in the morning and consistently perform all these activities.

Today, his book is converted to a Series. His various other books user the series are 'Miracle Morning Millionaires', 'The Miracle Morning for Salespeople', 'The Miracle Morning for Real Estate Agents', The Miracle Morning for Writers', 'The Miracle Morning for Entrepreneurs, 'The Miracle Morning for College Students', 'The Miracle Morning for Parents and Families', 'The Miracle Morning for Network Marketers', 'The Miracle Morning for Transforming Your Relationship', 'The Miracle Morning for Teachers', 'The Miracle Morning for Addiction Recovery', 'The Miracle Morning – Companion Planner', and much more.

Today, Hal Elrod is a successful motivational speaker, life coach, writer, and is one of the highest-rated keynote speakers in America. How this all this happened? It happened only because he decided to be consistent in his work. Performing these activities on a consistent basis will enhance the creativity and productivity of the individual. Surely, consistency can do Miracles.

2.4

The $1,00,000 Painting

One day, while Pablo Picasso, the world's most influential artist in the 20th century, was enjoying his evening meal at a restaurant. He got interrupted by a fan that handed over a paper to him and said, "Could you sketch something for me? I'll pay you for it. Tell your price". In response, Picasso pulled out a charcoal pencil from his pocket and swiftly sketched an image of a goat. The man reached out to collect the paper, but Picasso withheld it. He said, "You owe me $100,000. The man was outraged, "$100,000? Why? That took you only 30 minutes to draw". Picasso then crumpled up the paper and stuffed it into his jacket pocket and said, "You are wrong, it took me 30 years".

From the age of five years old, Picasso drew spontaneously. He drew on anything he could get his hands on and sketched everything he saw. To the naked eye, it may look like Picasso was an overnight success and a natural-born creative genius, but his story would say otherwise. It took nearly 20 years for his hard work to pay off and the breakthrough moment of success to arrive.

During his lifetime, Picasso produced an estimated 50,000 artworks, including 885 paintings, 1,228 sculptures, 2,880 ceramics, 12,000 drawings, and thousands of prints, tapestries, and rugs. In 1890, at the age of eight years old, Picasso created his first artwork, The Picador, and produced up to 50,000 artworks until he died at the age of 91 years old. This means, Picasso spent approximately 30,295 days working on his craft and produced an average of one new piece of artwork each day.

By the time he produced the breakthrough painting, Picasso would have spent nearly 20 years creating approximately 7,300 pieces of artwork. This is an incredible volume of work by any standard. Picasso's story stands in unambiguous contrast to the messages of instant results and overnight success. It's a humbling reminder that there are no secrets, magic pills, or shortcuts to success in life and work.

It was the consistent practice of Picasso by which he could draw a painting worth $1,00,000 in 30 seconds. We only see where people are today, but we fail to see the consistency and hard work that they have put in to reach this position. Picasso's story brings home the timeless ingredients of success through consistency, hard work, and patience.

2.5

Goal Post is Small

One of the best hockey players that the world and India has ever had, was Dhyan Chand. Not only did he make our country's name shine in International sports events, but the way he played hockey was so iconic, that the defenders would look as if they have no idea what's going on between the ball and his hockey stick. Chand played a pivotal role in India winning three consecutive Olympic gold medals in 1928, 1932, and 1936. His birth anniversary, 29th August, is celebrated as the National Sports Day in India and the President gives away awards such as Rajiv Gandhi Khel Ratna, Arjuna, and Dronacharya awards on this day.

Once, when Dhyan Chand was unable to score during a match, he argued with the match referee about the measurement of the goal post. To everyone's shock, Chand was right; the goal post was found to be small, it was a breach of the official minimum width prescribed as per international rules. How was he in a position to identify that the goal post was small? It was only through his constant practice and commitment to his job.

When we look back on his life, Dhyan Chand joined the Indian Army at the young age of 16 and took up hockey while he was still enrolled. Since Dhyan Singh used to practice a lot during the night, he was given the nickname 'Chand' by his fellow players; his practice sessions at night invariably coincided with the coming out of the moon. 'Chand' means moon in Hindi. Dhyan Chand would also practice on railway tracks by ensuring that the ball does not fall and hence learning the art of controlling and balancing the hockey ball.

During the 1928 Amsterdam Olympics, Dhyan Chand was the leading goal-scorer with 14 goals. A news report about India's victory said, "This is not a game of hockey, but magic. Dhyan Chand is, in fact, the magician of hockey".

Dhyan Chand's marvelous playing feared the officials in the Netherlands. This made them break his hockey stick just to check if there was a magnet inside. To honor Dhyan Chand, the residents of Vienna, Austria had set up a statue with four hands and four hockey sticks, depicting his mastery in the game. Adolf Hitler was so impressed by Dhyan Chand's stick work that he offered him German citizenship and the rank of Colonel in his army. This is a result of consistent hard work and nothing else.

2.6

Reading Leading

What is one common practice which most of the ultra-successful people do? The answer is 'Reading'. People like Warren Buffet, Elon Musk, and Mark Cuban are all titans of their industries. The one thing which all these people have been doing consistently over the years is 'Reading'.

Warren Buffett is one of the wealthiest and successful investors in the world. Throughout his teenage, he read voraciously. His daily reading list is comprised of at least five top-tier magazines and newspapers like the Wall Street Journal and Forbes. It's no wonder that he's got his finger on the pulse of the investment and business world.

Elon Musk, the CEO of Space X and Tesla (but more importantly, the man with the vision for the future of global society), grew up reading science fiction books. He said he was first introduced to the world of rocket science by reading books. And that he was only nine years old when he read the entire Encyclopedia. He also once said, "I was raised by books".

Mark Cuban, an incredibly successful businessman, investor, and television personality manifested his success by reading about successful people that came before him.

The information you provide yourself, with the books and articles you read, are the nutrients you feed your brain. This clearly shows what impact any consistent act can do to an individual. This is the simplest habit all successful people follow consistently and is the easiest habit for us to implement immediately.

2.7

4 AM

Haruki Murakami is a Japanese writer. His books and stories have been bestsellers in Japan as well as internationally, with his work being translated into 50 languages and selling millions of copies outside his native country. His work has received numerous awards, including the World Fantasy Award, the Frank O'Connor International Short Story Award, the Franz Kafka Prize, and the Jerusalem Prize. Steven Poole of 'The Guardian' praised Murakami as "among the world's greatest living novelists" for his works and achievements.

Before his career, as a writer took off, Haruki Murakami owned a small jazz club in Tokyo. After closing the club, he'd write, which often kept him up until dawn. But after he sold his business to become a full-time novelist, he and his wife changed their schedule dramatically.

In one of his interviews, he said, "When I'm in writing mode for a novel, I get up at four AM and work for five to six hours…. I go to bed at nine PM. I keep to this routine every day without variation". Haruki

Murakami is up before dawn and he's in bed shortly after dark. And he's maintained this routine since the '80s.

What's most important here is maintaining a consistent schedule, day in and day out, at least on the days that you're working. Maintain a consistent schedule; harness the power of routine and repetition by waking up and going to bed at the same time each day. Because of a consistent schedule, one is able to get less distracted and creativity increases simultaneously. Today Haruki Murakami has reached such great heights, only because of his consistent schedule.

Haruki Murakami has remained consistent for years together in following a particular schedule, which has significantly contributed to his success. In order to remain consistent, mental strength is very much necessary, and the real test of mental strength is consistency. If one wants to measure his mental strength then he should see how consistency is he in his important and difficult tasks.

Consistency is not a one-day activity; it is a lifelong process. If one has to achieve something significant in his life then he should continue to be consistent in every stage of his life. One should make consistency in his way of life.

2.8

Bowl Out

A 'Bowl Out' is used in limited-overs cricket to decide a match that would otherwise end in a tie. The procedure is similar to a penalty shootout in football. Five bowlers from each side deliver one ball each at unguarded wickets. As per the rule, if each team has hit the same number of wickets after the first five bowlers per side, the bowling continues and is decided by sudden death.

Before the introduction of the 'Super Over' in International Twenty20 Cricket, if a match ended with the scores level (either because both teams reached the same score after 20 overs, or the second team scored exactly the par score under the Duckworth-Lewis method), the tie was broken with a 'Bow Out'. The rule was implemented during the first T20 Cricket World Cup in 2007. On, 14th September 2007, India was playing Pakistan in one of the league matches. The match ended with the scores level by both the teams as both the teams scored 141 runs in 20 overs. And as per the rule, the winner had to be decided through a 'Bowl Out'. No one expected that a 'Bowl Out' will decide the outcome of a game.

The five bowlers used by the India cricket team was RP Singh, S

THE POWER OF CONSISTENCY

Sreesanth, Ajit Agarkar, Irfan Pathan, and Harbhajan Singh. But when it came to 'Bowl Out', the five bowlers which were used were Virender Sehwag, Harbhajan Singh, Robin Uthappa, Irfan Pathan, and S Sreesanth. Ajit Agarkar was the most senior bowler and RP Singh was the opening bowler, but both of them were not considered for 'Bowl Out'. Whereas, Virender Sehwag and Robin Uthappa are recognized opening batsmen and not regular bowlers, but they were considered for 'Bowl Out'. On the other hand, Pakistan used the same five bowlers who were used in the match; they were Mohammad Asif, Umar Gul, Yasir Arafat, Sohail Tanvir, and Shahid Afridi.

From India's side, Virender Sehwag bowled the first ball and he hit the wickets and from Pakistan's side Yasir Arafat bowled the first ball and he missed hitting the wickets, and the score was 1-0. From India, the second ball was bowled by Harbhajan Singh who hit the wickets, and from Pakistan, it was Umar Gul who missed hitting the wickets, and not the score was 2-0. From India, the third delivery was bowled by Robin Uthappa who hit the wickets, and from Pakistan, it was Shahid Afridi who had to hit the wickets to keep the match alive, but he also missed the wickets and the score was 3-0 and India went on to win the match, and the remaining two balls were not bowled.

What was the reason why India opted for two batsmen who were not regular bowlers for 'Bowl Out', who went on to win the match for India, just after the third ball in 'Bowl Out'? The first Twenty20 Cricket World Cup had 'Bowl Out' and India had never practiced 'Bowl Out'. The team decided that every time they go for practice, they would do 'Bowl Out', either before the warm-up or after the warm-up, because there may come across a situation, where they would have to do a 'Bowl Out'.

The 'Bowl Out' practice was like a fun activity, but at the same time, they had decided that whoever hits the wicket most number of times, they will be the ones who will be used, if the situation arises. It was nothing like, it is a 'Bowl Out' and it is the job of the blowers to do it. They decided to keep doing it every day and whoever has the most consistent record with the best hit ratio will be the ones who will be used. Virender Sehwag and Robin Uthappa were selected because they were the most consistent in the team when it comes to hitting the wicket.

Thus, consistency pays off and helps a team win a close nail-biting match. It is not skill, talent, or professionalism which will lead a person or team to succeed, but it is consistency which will lead someone to success. Later India won all the other matches in the tournament and went on to win the first International Twenty20 Cricket World Cup.

2.9

23 Golds

Focusing on a single task with an unwavering dedication for years is a challenge. For Michael Phelps, who was diagnosed with ADHD (Attention Deficit Hyperactivity Disorder), when he was a child. ADHD is a complex neurodevelopmental disorder that impacts a person's ability to exert age-appropriate self-control. But once he was encouraged to take up swimming at the age of seven, he discovered his love for the sport and subsequently made it his life's goal to become the best swimmer ever.

On weekends, there was no practice. So he decided to add Saturdays to it. Because that means, 52 weeks X 6 hours is 312 hours more in the year. Then he thought, why not practice on Sundays as well, because that would add another 312 hours in the year. That's the kind of commitment he had to practice consistently.

Finally, Phelps trained six hours a day, seven days a week, 365 days a year, for almost two decades. He never once missed a day of practice, not Sundays, not birthdays, nor holidays like Christmas, unless injured. He wanted to be the best and he made it happen through sheer hard work.

Three years after winning six gold and 2 bronze medals at the 2004 Athens Olympics, Michael Phelps announced that he would beat the record of most first-place finishes, which was 7, in a single Olympics at the 2008 Beijing games. His remarks were met with mockery and scorn by people who criticized his bravado; after all, winning eight gold medals in a single Olympics sounds far-fetched. But, he took that as a challenge and consistently practiced for the next four years. In the 2008 Beijing Olympics, he went on to win 8 gold medals, creating a world record, which aspiring Olympians dream of beating.

Today, Michael Phelps is the most decorated Olympian of all time. He became the most felicitated Olympian in all history by backing an incredible 28 medals haul (23 golds, 3 silvers, and 2 bronzes) his record looks poised to remain unbroken for years. How was all this possible? It was only possible with consistent practice. This is what consistency can do even when one is diagnosed with hyperactivity and impulsiveness.

2.10

Squeeze – Shape – Cut – Fry

Vada started disappearing from Indian homes because it is one of the most difficult snacks to make at home. There are three significant challenges in making the Vada. First, we need to use the right combination of ingredients to getting the Vada batter right. Second, it is a messy job, as the Vada batter is as sticky as glue. Third, to make Vada from the batter, as we need to get the rights size and shape.

A company by name 'ID Fresh Food', started in 2005, based in Bengaluru, headed by P C Mustafa, wanted to solve this century-old problem and they worked hard consistently for three years to solve the problem. The process was not easy, but they never lost hope. Many in the team member also suggested dropping the project in between, but he was confident about it. They constantly worked hard to solve the homemakers' problem.

The solution was 'ID Vada Pack', which has a spout, which shapes batter into Vadas, with the hole. Not the process is very simple, just Squeeze –

Shape – Cut – Fry. Now, the process has no mess, no stress, just crispy Vadas. It helps to make homemade Vadas that are shaped, sized, just like an expert made Vadas, without touching the batter, and most importantly, with a proper hole in the middle. It is also 100% natural, no chemical, no preservatives, nothing artificial in it. Now it takes one minute to make Vada at home. Today, Vada making is no more an 'Art'; it is a 'Science'.

Today, 'ID Fresh Foods' is valued at 1,000 crores. P C Mustafa is listed by Forbes India as 'Tycoons of Tomorrow'. He is the youngest recipient of the Distinguished Alumni Awards in the history of IIM Bangalore.

2.11

One Percent

In 1986, the Los Angeles Lakers had one of the most talented basketball teams ever assembled, but they are rarely remembered that way. The team started the 1985 – 1986 NBA season with an astounding 29 – 5 record. People were saying that they might be the best team in the history of basketball. Surprisingly, the Lakers stumbled in the 1986 playoffs and suffered a season-ending defeat in the Western Conference Finals. The "best team in the history of basketball" didn't even play for the NBA championship.

After that blow, Coach Pat Riley was tired of hearing about how much talent his players had and about how many promises his team held. He didn't want to see flashes of brilliance followed by a gradual fade-in performance. He wanted the Lakers to play up to their potential, night after night. In the summer of 1986, he created a plan to do exactly that, a system that he called the Career Best Effort (CBE) Program.

In the CBE Program, the current performance of the calculated using various aspects such as points, rebounds, assists, steals, turnovers, and total minutes played. After the final score was calculated the players were asked to improve their output by at least 1 percent over the course of the season, which could happen through consistent practice.

The Lakers rolled out CBE in October 1986. Eight months later, they were NBA champions. The following year, Pat Riley led his team to another title as the Lakers became the first team in twenty years to win back-to-back NBA championships. Afterward, he said, "Sustaining an effort is the most important thing for any enterprise. The way to be successful is to learn how to do things right, then do them the same way every time". This is what consistency can do. There exists a narrow gap that separates the good performance from the great performance. And that narrow gap is separated by consistency and small habits.

2.12
13 Virtues and 52 Weeks

Benjamin Franklin was an American polymath and one of the Founding Fathers of the United States. Franklin was a leading writer, printer, political philosopher, politician, Freemason, postmaster, scientist, inventor, humorist, civic activist, statesman, and diplomat. As a scientist, he was a major figure in the American Enlightenment and the history of physics for his discoveries and theories regarding electricity. As an inventor, he is known for the lightning rod, bifocals, and the Franklin stove, among other inventions. He founded many civic organizations, including the Library Company, Philadelphia's first fire department, and the University of Pennsylvania.

He attributes his success to consistently practicing 13 core life virtues, to the best of his ability. He believed that by living those virtues, he had done everything he could to put himself in a position to be on the good side of the unexpected events of life. He actually had an incredible system for working on those virtues, which I want to talk about today.

THE POWER OF CONSISTENCY

He carried around a card in his pocket that depicted a simple table with seven columns and 13 rows on it. Each column on this card represented a day of the week, Sunday to Saturday. Each row on this card represented one of the 13 virtues that he wanted to work on. The 13 virtues were Temperance, Silence, Order, Resolution, Frugality, Industry, Sincerity, Justice, Moderation, Cleanliness, Tranquility, Chastity, and Humility.

He tracked and reflected upon each day. His goal was to improve himself with regard to each virtue so that over time he was a better person in that regard and by being a better overall person and was more open to opportunities.

During the day, he might glance at these virtues a time or two to keep them fresh in his mind. At the end of each day, however, he'd pull out a pen and go through those virtues, asking himself if he has actually practiced them during the day and marking the box if he had done so. His goal was to fill in as many boxes as possible, and each week, he would start a new with a fresh blank chart.

He had 13 variations of the charts, which he cycled through every 13 weeks. On top of each variation of the card was listed one virtue, which was the main one he wanted to practice that week, along with a brief description of that virtue. For example, one week, he might really focus on frugality, while the next week might particularly focus on temperance. He would reflect on and record his success with all 13 virtues each day, but he would intentionally focus on just one virtue each week.

A final key part of his practice is that he would review the cards as a whole at the end of each week, evaluating which virtues were successful that week, which ones were not, and which areas really needed focus and improvement in his life. He would also review them as a set, and thus with 13 cards to review, that roughly covers three months. After 13 weeks were over, he would again repeat the activity; by this, he would have practiced each skill for 4 weeks in a year, which would cover 52 weeks of the year.

He found himself naturally practicing them more than he once did, which made him into a better-rounded and successful person and a better participant in society, which he attributed to being a healthy part of the success that he found in almost every attribute of life.

The key thing to always remember with a process like this takes time. People always want immediate results that appear like magic. Improving ourselves takes time, and then it takes even more time for the effects of that improvement to propagate out into our life. The key thing with this is to remember that we will get getting better, little by little. If we strive to be a little better than the day before, we will always be heading in the right direction, and given enough time, that change will be visible.

Once, we have defined a set of virtues or skills, we need to work on them consistently so that we can witness some positive results. Then, we should also review our work on a regular periodic basis. Over a period of time, these virtues become ingrained in one's character.

This really is a simple yet brilliant system for genuine self-improvement. It can help our change your character as a whole or help us bring about true lasting improvement in specific areas of our life. The key is to trust the process, be consistent, keep doing this over a long period of time and we find ourselves in a better place.

2.13

Block and Punch

In Martial Arts, the students are trained to Block and Punch every day. Every day, before they begin their actual training, they begin the training with Block and Punch activity. They do this practice consistently for months and years together. How much ever experienced they become, they would always begin the training with Block and Punch activity.

The reason behind doing this practice consistently is because it comes in their reflex action. The moment somebody attacks them, even when they are sleeping, they would block and punch. Even when they are casually sitting and someone would attack them, then they would immediately Block and Attack them. Due to consistent practice, it becomes a habit and settles in the subconscious mind.

The function of the subconscious mind is to store and retrieve data. Its job is to ensure that we respond exactly the way we are programmed. Our subconscious mind makes everything we say and do fit a pattern consistent with our self-concept, our 'master program'. This is why doing activities consistently are so effective we can actually reprogram our own thought patterns by slipping in positive and success-oriented sound bites.

Our subconscious mind is subjective. It does not think or reason independently; it merely obeys the commands it receives from our conscious mind. Just as our conscious mind can be thought of as the gardener, planting seeds, our subconscious mind can be thought of as the garden, or fertile soil, in which the seeds germinate and grow. This is the reason why one should perform activities on a consistent basis.

Our subconscious mind also practices homeostasis in our mental realm, by keeping us thinking and acting in a manner consistent with what we have done and said in the past. All our habits of thinking and acting are stored in your subconscious mind. Thus, our subconscious mind can be programmed if we do activities in a consistent manner.

2.14

Super 30

Super 30 is an Indian educational program that started in Patna, India under the banner of Ramanujan School of Mathematics. It was founded by Anand Kumar, a mathematics teacher, and Abhayanand, the former D.G.P of Bihar. The program selects 30 talented candidates each year from economically underprivileged sections of Indian society and trains them for the JEE. Anand Kumar, and his school, has been the subject of several smear campaigns, some of which have been carried in Indian media sources.

In 2002, Abhayanand and Anand Kumar started Super 30 with the plan to select 30 talented students from economically impoverished sections who could not afford IIT coaching. These 30 students were then prepared to pass IIT-JEE examinations. Anand Kumar's mother, Jayanti Devi, volunteered to cook for the students while Anand Kumar, Abhayanand, and other teachers tutored them. The students were also provided study materials and lodging for a year free of cost.

In the first year of the coaching, 18 out of 30 students made it to IIT. The following year, application numbers soared due to the popularity of the program, and a written examination was conducted to select 30 students. In 2004, 22 out of 30 students qualified for IIT-JEE, increasing the popularity of the program which attracted even more applications. In 2005, 26 out of 30 students cleared the IIT-JEE exam, while 28 in 2006, this despite the fact that IIT changed the examination structure.

Anand Kumar continued to constantly work hard and the following year 28 more students cleared the IIT-JEE, and in 2008, all of the Super 30 students cleared the IIT-JEE, after which Abhayanand quit Super 30 saying 'the experiment is over'. Some of Anand Kumar's former students joined as Super 30 teachers and in 2009 and 2010 all 30 students again qualified the IIT JEE exams. In subsequent years the success rates from the 30 students were: 2011 (24 passed), 2012 (27 passed), 2013 (28 passed), 2014 (27 passed), 2015 (25 passed), and in 2016 (28 passed). In 2017, all Super 30 candidates made it to the IIT-JEE. In 2018, 26 of the 30 students cleared the exam.

Time Magazine included Super 30 in its list of The Best of Asia 2010. The organization also received praise from US President Barack Obama's special envoy Rashad Hussain, who termed it the 'best' institute in the country. Newsweek Magazine included Super 30 in its list of Four Most Innovative Schools in the World. He was awarded the Maulana Abul Kalam Azad Shiksha Puraskar in November 2010, the highest award given by the Bihar state government in the field of education. He received the prestigious Nachiketa Award at the International Principals Educational Conference 2019.

All these achievements were only possible due to the consistent and focused effort of Anand Kumar. He was not only creating 30 geniuses at a time, but he was changing lives, thousands at a time, because when a child studies, then his whole family and their future generation changes forever.

2.15

Computer Boy

When this boy was in 7th grade and was an intelligent child. His father pulled him out of public school and got him admitted into a private school of the elite of Seattle called 'Lakeside'. The next year the mothers of the school children did a rummage sale for charity, and out of the collections, they donated a computer terminal to the lakeside school.

That was pretty advanced technology in the year 1968 because Bill Joy, the founder of Sun Microsystems, got access to a computer terminal in 1971 when he was in college but this boy got it in the school itself, as an 8th grader in 1968. He along with his friends made that computer room their living place. They found it so fascinating; they were spending all their time there. However it was connected to a mainframe computer in Seattle, and time-sharing in those days was very expensive. The consequence was that the money the mothers had deposited ran out fast. They deposited more, that also ran out.

Fortunately, there was a company called C-Cube (Computer Center

Corporation). It came to know of these kids and told them that they would give them free computer time, if they would do quality control, testing for their programs. So, the boy again got access to a computer and he was spending hours upon it. Later, C-Cube ran out of business and again they were denied access.

Another company came along called ISI (Information Systems Incorporated). They came to know of these kids who were interested in computers. They wanted to develop software for their payroll system. If they do it, they would have access to their computers. The again pounced upon it but after a few months, the boy and his friends, they stole the password, crashed the system, because of which they were thrown out.

Later, the boy came to know that the University of Washington in Seattle gives free access to the computer in the early morning hours from 3 am to 6 am. He began utilizing that slot. After a few months, another company called TWR, they needed some programming, for their power plants, and these kids were becoming better and better at computers and came to know of them. They contacted the school and said that they would offer a summer project to them if they were willing to do such and such thing. Again the boy got an opportunity to work on it.

And the consequence of all of this was that by the time this boy reached Harvard, he already has 10,000 hours of coding experience with him. The boy is no one but Bill Gates. To say that he just dropped out of college and started Microsoft is an understatement. He worked consistently and strived hard to reach that point. Success did not fall into our laps, but it comes from consistency.

2.16

Piston Ring to Motorcycle

Mr. Soichiro Honda, the founder of Honda Automobile Empire, was not born with a golden spoon in his mouth in Japan. He was born in a lower-middle-class family. He had an inspiration burning in him to do something that would make a difference.

He went to an engineering school and designed a prototype for piston rings and went and presented it to Toyota as a superior design, but they rejected it. After that, he became a laughing stock of his colleagues and friends. However, he was inspired, so he did not give up and made another design and it got selected. So, Toyota gave him an order and they extended him the capital to set up his factory for piston rings.

When he got his factory done, there was an earthquake in Japan and the factory collapsed. He did not give up and he was about to make it the second time, Japan entered into the Second World War and cement was short in supply. He did not give up, he found a new way to make cement, and with the help of that he set up his factory. However, by that time America entered the war and they bombed his factory, as they were bombing Japan.

He was still inspired and was consistently striving towards his goal. During the Second World War, the planes were different. Once the fuel was used, to lighten the plane, they would throw the gasoline tank. So, the ground was filled with all these gasoline tanks of the American bomber planes. He used these gasoline tanks to make his factory again for the 3rd time. His factory was ready, by then Japan has lost the war fuel was in short supply and people did not have the fuel to drive Toyota cars, due to which there were no orders for piston rings.

One day he got a brain wave while riding his bicycle. He set a motor into the bicycle and it was the first motorcycle. When he drove around the neighborhood, his friends looked at it and requested him to that for them as well. Then he made about 20 motorcycles, he thought he had a marketable idea, but he did not have the money to produce motorcycles. He did not give up and got a list of 800 bicycle stockists of Japan and handwrote notes to 5000 of them. Out of 1800 responded a little bit of capital. With the help of this capital, he set up his motorcycle factory.

The first motorcycle he made was very big and it was a failure. He never gave it and made a smaller model, which was called 'The Super Cub' and it was an immediate success and after that, there was no looking back.

During his time, Honda Corporation employed 1,00,000 people worldwide and now it is even beyond. Finally, the key ingredient for success was 'consistency', which was displayed by Mr. Soichiro Honda throughout his life.

2.17

The Mountain Man

For years, he was called a madman for toiling away on the rocks. But Dashrath Manjhi was not crazy. His quest to break a path through a small mountain to benefit the entire village is now legendary because he carved an entire road with hand tools, working for 22 years.

Manjhi started off his extraordinary task in 1960 after his wife was injured while trekking up the side of one of the rocky footpaths. To reach the nearest hospital, he had to travel around the mountains, around 70 km.

The laborer from Gehlour Hills in Bihar, India wanted his people to have easier access to doctors, schools, and opportunities. Armed with only a sledgehammer, chisel, and crowbar, he single-handedly began carving a road through the 300-foot mountain that isolated his village from the nearest town.

People told Manjhi that he wouldn't be able to do it as he was a poor man who just needs to earn and eat. He sold the family's three goats to buy the hammer and chisels and worked every day on the project to make it successful. After plowing fields for others in the morning, he would work on his road all evening and throughout the night.

He toiled from 1960 to 1982, having developed his own technique. He burned firewood on the rocks and then sprinkled water on the heated surface which cracked the boulders making it possible to reduce them to rubble.

He carved a path 110 m long (360 feet), 9.1 m (30 feet) wide, and 7.7 m (25 feet) deep through a ridge of hills using only a hammer and chisel. After 22 years of work, Dashrath shortened travel between the Atri and Wazirganj blocks of Gaya town in Bihar from 55 km to 15 km.

For his feat, Manjhi became popularly known as the 'Mountain Man'. The Bihar government also proposed his name for the Padma Shree award in 2006 in the social service sector. A stamp featuring Dashrath Manjhi was released by India Post in the 'Personalities of Bihar' series on 26th December 2016. He was given a state funeral by the Government of Bihar when he died in 2007. A documentary and a movie were also made in his life.

What is the secret of this achievement? No prize for giving the right answer. It was pure consistent hard work for 22 years. Thus, if we want to achieve something extraordinary then consistency is only the formula.

THE POWER OF CONSISTENCY

There are no shortcuts to success; one consistent hard work is the way forward. Where there is a will, there is a way.

2.18

What is Your Job?

Rajiv Bajaj, Managing Director of Bajaj Auto met a Japanese Professor Yamaguchi. When he met him, he was Vice President Products of Bajaj Auto and was heading R&D and Engineering and was working hard on the Pulsar. The professor asked him what his job was, and Rajiv replied that he was Vice President Products. The professor replied stating that it was his designation and not his job.

The professor again asked him what his job was. Rajiv replied that his job was to develop motorcycles. The professor replied, so you are working on the drawing board. Rajiv replied that he was not actually working on the drawing board.

The professor again asked then what your job was. Rajiv replied that my job is to make a design that is very efficient for manufacturing. Professor replied that not I understand, working on the machine is your job. Rajiv replied, no I don't work on the machine myself.

Then the professor again asked what his job was. Rajiv became a little anxious and said that his job was to develop such beautiful motorcycles that all the boys should be wanting to buy it and maybe some girls as well. The professor replied, now I understand that you are a salesman in a dealer's workshop. Rajiv replied, no, I am not doing that as well.

Then the professor looked at him and said that you don't design, you don't make, you don't sell, and then what is your job. After some time he smiled and he said that you are a manager and 'talking' is your job. You don't do anything with your own hands. At least a surgeon, a cricketer, a musician, a chef use their hands.

Then Rajiv asked him to please tell him what his job was. The professor said that 'improvement' is your job. Every day you must ask yourself that can you create an environment in your company so that everybody who comes there is motivated to do better than he did yesterday. If you can create this type of empowerment and enablement of your employees, then you are doing your job.

Ultimately, the lesson which can be learned from this real-life incident is to be improving consistently. Even if a person is at the helm of affairs in an organisation, his main job should be to ensure that people who are working under him are improving continuously, as they are the only thing which would make the individual and the organisation different from the other.

2.19

3 Kilometer in 30 Years

During the rainy season, the water falling from the mountains used to flow into the river which used to bother Bhuiyan following which he thought of carving out a canal.

He carved out a 3-kilometer long canal to take rainwater coming down from nearby hills to fields of his village, Kothilawa in Lahthua area of Gaya in Bihar. IT is surrounded by dense forest and mountains, about 80 km away from Gaya district headquarters. This village is marked as a refuge for Maoists.

It took him 30 years to dig this canal which takes the water to a pond in the village. He dug out the canal single-handedly in Gaya. A lot of people, animals will benefit from his work. The water will be used to irrigate the fields as well. It has become a means of livelihood for the people in Gaya as the water is used for farming and animal husbandry.

For 30 years, he would go to the nearby jungle to tend his cattle and dig out the canal. No one joined him in this endeavor. The people staying in his village were going to cities to earn a livelihood but he decided to stay back.

He could only achieve the extraordinary by being consistent for a span of 30 years.

2.20

It Will Never Fail You

Introduction

Consistency will never fail you. No person in the world who has been consistent in a particular field has failed. Consistency is the secret to avoid failure and be successful. Consistency is a path that will help a person achieve something which looks impossible. The following are a few stories of success that were a result of consistency.

1. Village Boy to IIM-Bangalore

P C Mustafa was a village boy from Kerala. Once, on his trip to Bannerghatta Zoo, he saw IIM-B and dreamt of earning a place in the IIM-B campus one day. He was a below-average student. He was rejected in many campus interviews as he was not able to perform well in analytical areas. He knew that he needed high analytical skills to study at a prestigious institute at IIM-B. So, he consistently practiced for 2 hours daily after the Morning Prayer and finally, he was selected for the PGSEM Programme. Today, P C Mustafa is the CEO and Co-Founder of iD Fresh Food.

2. Self Balancing

Two students from IIT Kharagpur and IIT Madras came up with an idea to come up with a 2 wheeler which would completely transform the experience of riding a 2 wheeler, by creating a self-balancing vehicle and co-founded a company called Liger Mobility. The rolled-up their sleeves and got going with some physics, maths, and a whole bunch of other stuff. After thousands of lines of code, several prototypes, and two years of consistent hard work, they achieved what they had originally set out for.

3. 1000 Videos – 1000 Days

Nuseir Yassin a video blogger and a Youtuber. He created 1000 daily informative 1-minute videos on Facebook under the page, Nas Daily, which was almost for 3 years. He decided to be consistent in his work. His consistency paid off, he went on to become popular across the globe and his Youtube channel 'Nas Daily' has more than 1.6 million (16 lakh) subscribers as of 1st September 2020.

4. Eight PM to Eight AM

Thirukumaran, Co-Founder and CEO Ninjacart, and his team slept in the sabzi mandis (vegetable markets) consistently for a period of 3 to 4 months to understand what really happens in the market. As the wholesale market would mainly work in the night, they would reach the market at eight in the evening and stay till eight or nine in the morning. Today, Ninjacart is India's largest B2B Fresh Produce Supply Chain Company, which basically helps farmers to directly sell their crops to the end retailers. It has also notched up a delivery accuracy rate of 99.88 percent.

5. Practice + Theory + Sleep

Nadia Comaneci was a gymnast who had a unique daily schedule. She would practice for 16 hours, have a theory session for 4 hours, and would sleep for 4 hours; she would repeat this schedule consistently every day. Her consistency leads to her great heights. She went on to become a five-time Olympic gold medalist, all in individual events. She was the first gymnast to be awarded a perfect score of 10.0 at the Olympic Games, and then, at the same Games (1976 Summer Olympics in Montreal), she received six more perfect 10s en route to winning three gold medals. At the 1980 Summer Olympics in Moscow, she won two more gold medals and attained two more perfect 10s. During her career, she won nine Olympic medals and four World Artistic Gymnastics Championship medals. She is one of the world's best-known gymnasts and is credited with popularizing the sport around the globe. In 2000, she was named as one of the Athletes of the 20th Century by the Laureus World Sports Academy.

6. Twelve Hours Every Day

Lance Armstrong was a professional road racing cyclist. He used to train himself for 12 hours every day. He won the World Championship in 1993, the Clasica de San Sebastian in 1995, Tour DuPont in 1995 and 1996, and a handful of stage victories in Europe, including stage 8 of the 1993 Tour de France and stage 18 of the 1995 Tour de France. In 1996, he was diagnosed with a potentially fatal metastatic testicular cancer. He returned to cycling in 1998 and was a member of the US Discovery team between 1998 and 2005 when he won his Tour de France titles, as well as a bronze medal in the 2000 Summer Olympics. This was only because of his consistent practice.

7. Druvh Rathe

Dhruv Rathee is a Youtuber, who makes informative videos on various political, social, economic, and religious issues. His YouTube channel has more than 4.2 million (42 lakh) subscribers as of 1st September 2020. His YouTube channel is way ahead in subscription and viewership when compared to various mainstream channels and news portals which have a large number of employees. His videos become viral on various social media platforms and are viewed by people across the globe. He was able to achieve this in a very short span of time because of unique content and consistency. It is easy to make a good video and make it viral, but it is hard to be consistent in making good videos.

III

Stories and Events

3.1

Hare and Tortoise

Once upon a time a turtle and a hare had an argument about who was faster. They decided to settle the argument with a race. The tortoise and hare both agreed on a route and started off the race. The rabbit shot ahead and ran briskly for some time, then seeing that he was far ahead of the turtle, he thought that he could sit under a tree for some time and relax before continuing the race.

He sat under the tree and soon fell asleep. The tortoise moved steadily on overtook him a soon finished the race, emerging as the undisputed champion. The hare woke up and realized that he had lost the race. The moral of the story was 'Slow and Steady Wins the Race'.

We have read this story in our childhood and have learned that 'Slow and Steady Wins the Race'. But the story has many other dimensions as well. One of the significant learning from the story is the positive impact of being consistent, which was exhibited by tortoise.

When we are consistent, that creates momentum. That momentum creates progress. Progress creates self-confidence. The self-confidence starts shaping a new, more resourceful, and empowering identity. And with this new identity comes the ability to create lasting change in our life.

We need to take our goals and chop them up into small daily minimum quotas. Then, start obsessing about executing on them every single day. Initially consistently looks like it is yielding no result, but in the long run, it pays off. It is not speed which is important, but it is consistency which is important to win.

3.2

Cracked Pot

A young woman worked for a merchant who lived on top of a hill. She worked as the merchant's laundress and every day she had to walk down the hill to collect water from a stream. She had two pots to carry water, which she hung upon a pole she could carry over her shoulders. With time one of her pot got a slender crack along its side. She observed the cracks on the pot and decided she could still use it.

Every day, the woman carried those pots down the hill to the stream, filled them to the brim, and walked back up the hill, balancing the pole across her shoulders. By the time she reached the house, the cracked pot would be only half full while the other pot delivered a full portion of water.

The cracked pot glanced at the other pot and saw water filled to the top, and it began to feel isolated. The full pot was proud of its accomplishment while the cracked pot felt ashamed and miserable that it was able to accomplish only half of what it was meant to.

After a few years of what the cracked pot perceived to be a failure, it spoke to the lady. "I apologize for my flaws. The crack on my side has made me useless. I spill half of the water. I'm of no good", the pot said.

The lady felt sorry for the old cracked pot and she said, "But pot, you don't understand, you haven't been paying attention. Look around you. As we return to the master's house, I want you to look at the path we traverse".

The next time when the lady carried the water up to the hill, the pot carefully observed the path up the hill. For the first time the pot stopped looking inward and instead looked out. On his side of the trail the pot noticed beautiful flowers growing in abundance, while the other side was still dry.

As the woman reached the top of the hill, she asked "Did you notice the beautiful flowers on the path? They are only on your side of the path. I had always known about your cracks and I took advantage of it to water those beautiful flowers along the way. Without you being just the way you are, the path uphill would not have this beauty".

The cracked pot was overjoyed. All its sadness was gone. He understood that the very thing he thought to be his flaws turned out to be a blessing for the flowers along the path. Every one of us is unique and we have our own flaws, but if we are consistent, we can create a deep impact.

3.3

Fighting Cancer

Japanese cell biologist Yoshinori Ohsumi won the Nobel Prize in Medicine in 2016 for his research on how cells recycle and renew their content, a process called autophagy.

Autophagy is a process where during starvation; cells break down proteins and other cell components and use them for energy. During autophagy, cells destroy viruses and bacteria and get rid of damaged structures. It's a process that is critical for cell health, renewal, and survival.

Fasting activates autophagy, which helps slow down the aging process and has a positive impact on cell renewal. The process of Autophagy helps a body fight different kinds of bacteria and viruses including cancer viruses as well as recycle these bacteria and all kinds of viruses from the body instantly. There is also a large body of research that connects fasting with improved blood sugar control, reduced inflammation, weight loss, and improved brain function.

As research into autophagy has expanded, it has become clear that it is not simply a response to starvation. It also contributes to a range of physiological functions, such as stopping cancer cells and aging, eliminating pathogens, and cleaning the insides of cells.

While Yoshinori Ohsumi was presenting his discovery to the people and top Japanese scientists around him, someone asked, what is the ideal time for Autophagy to fight cancer bacteria? Yoshinori Ohsumi answered that it needs 8 hours to 14 hours of starvation for approximately 25 to 28 days a month every year to completely wipe out cancer viruses from the body. Thus, when people are consistent in fasting, it works and gives the result. This is the magic of being consistent.

Muslims all around the world fast 29 to 30 days a month every year. That comes with starvation and is stretched from 8 hours to 14+ hours depending on the longest and shortest fast around the world. Fasting during the month of Ramadan is ideal for Autophagy's process to happen, which helps to fight in cancer viruses. Yoshinori Ohsumi told that Muslim's way of fasting is an ideal thing that will help this process to happen.

3.4

Water Torture

Take a water bottle, make a small hole on the bottle cap, and place it on the table to drip water drop by drop on your forehead. This seems like a harmless exercise because it is just a drop of water, but each of these droplets of water represents a small, tiny irritation that can be easily ignored.

After two hours of sitting like this we will physically won't be able to take it anymore, we will go insane from the constant water drops, especially if they are cold. This is popularly known as 'Chines Water Torture'. It may also be characterised by the inconsistent pattern of water drips. People use this method to torture people. This form of torture was first described under a different name by Hippolytus de Marsiliis in Italy in the 15th or 16th century.

When a bottle of water is slashed on our head at once, it might not give us a lot of trouble, but when the same waterfalls in drops, it irritates. That's how effective small droplets of water can be. Small stress points, small droplets of water, when sustained over a period of time, can be quite powerful. It is just a drop of water, which has no significance, but when it falls consistently, it becomes irritating and becomes torture.

3.5

Sharpen Your Saw

Once upon a time, there were two woodcutters named. They were often at loggerheads over who chopped more wood. So one day, they decided to hold a competition to determine the winner. The rules were simple, whoever produce the most wood in a day wins.

So the next day morning, both of them took up their positions in the forest and started chopping away in their fastest possible speed. This lasted for an hour before the first woodcutter suddenly stopped. When the first woodcutter realized that there was no chopping sound from his opponent's side, he thought that he must be tired already and he continued to cut down his trees with double the pace.

A quarter of an hour passed, and the first woodcutter heard his opponent chopping again and both of them carried on synchronously. The first woodcutter was starting to feel weary when the chopping from the second woodcutter stopped once again. Feeling motivated and smelling victory close by, the first woodcutter continued on, with a smile on his face.

This went on the whole day. Every hour, the second woodcutter would stop chopping for 10 minutes while the first woodcutter kept going relentlessly. So, when the competition came to an end, the first woodcutter was absolutely confident that he would take the triumph.

But to his astonishment, the second woodcutter had actually cut down more wood. How did this even happen? "How could you have chopped down more trees than me? I heard you stop working every hour for around 10 minutes". The second woodcutter replied by saying, "Every time I stopped work, while you were still chopping down trees, I was sharpening my axe and this helped me cut more trees than you".

What was the difference between two woodcutters? The first woodcutter only focused on cutting the trees, but the second woodcutter focused on consistently 'sharpening his saw', which helped him to become more productive than the first woodcutter. This is the magic that consistency can create.

IV

Concepts

4.1

5 Dimensions of Improvement

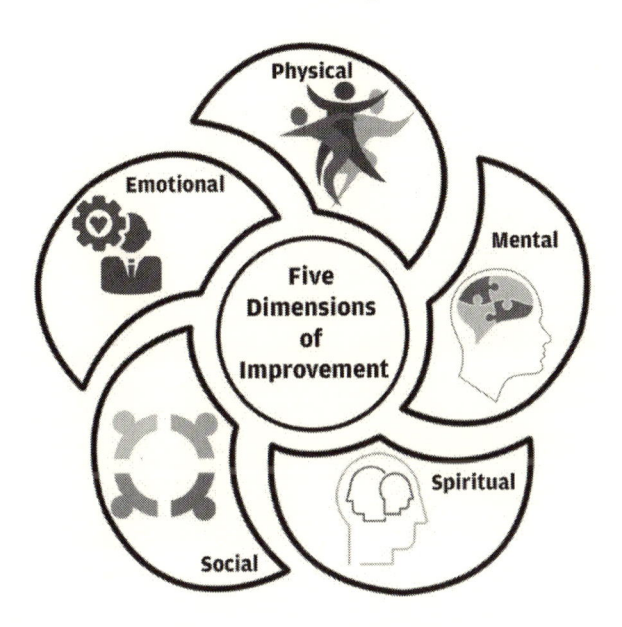

Introduction

In order to keep ourselves productive, we need to consistently work on five aspects of our life. These five aspects are physical, mental, spiritual, social, and emotional. Even if anyone aspect is neglected, or is not given consistent focus, then it will hamper the productivity of the individual. Thus, having a balanced program for constant self-development in the five aspects of our life is very much necessary.

Aspects

The following is the detailed explanation:

1. Physical

Physical wellness encompasses a variety of healthy behaviors including adequate exercise, proper nutrition, and abstaining from harmful habits such as drug use and alcohol abuse. It means learning about and identifying symptoms of the disease, getting regular medical checkups, and protecting ourselves from injuries and harm. Developing such healthy habits today will not only add years to our life but will enhance the enjoyment and quality of those years. The following are a few tips for physical wellness:

- Exercise/walk daily.
- Get adequate rest.
- Sleep well.
- Eat a variety of healthy foods.
- Avoid over eating.
- Avoid smoking and consumption of alcohol.

2. Mental

The intellectual dimension encourages creative, stimulating mental activities. Our minds need to be continually inspired and exercised just as our bodies do. People who possess a high level of intellectual wellness have an active mind and continue to learn. An intellectually well person uses the resources available to expand one's knowledge and improve skills. Keeping up-to-date on current events and participating in activities that arouse our minds are also important. The following are a few tips for mental wellness:

- Reading.
- Taking a course or workshop.
- Learning a language.
- Spend time with people who challenge you intellectually.

3. Spiritual

Spiritual wellness involves possessing a set of guiding beliefs, principles, or values that help give direction to one's life. It encompasses a high level of faith, hope, and commitment to our individual beliefs that provide a sense of meaning and purpose. It is a willingness to seek meaning and purpose in human existence, to question everything, and to appreciate the things which cannot be readily explained or understood. A spiritually well person seeks harmony between what lies within as well as the forces outside. The following are a few tips for spiritual wellness:

- Pray regularly.
- Always be conscious of God.
- Spend time alone and introspect on our life and things around you.
- Be inquisitive and curious.
- Listen with our heart.

4. Social

Social wellness refers to our ability to interact successfully in our global community and to live up to the expectations and demands of our personal roles. This means learning good communication skills, developing intimacy with others, and creating a support network of friends and family members. Social wellness includes showing respect for others and ourselves. Contributing to our community and to the world builds a sense of belonging. The following are a few tips for social wellness:

- Cultivate healthy relationships.
- Contribute and help the people in the community.
- Use our talents and skills for the betterment of the society.
- Never break ties, especially with close relatives.

5. Emotional

Emotional wellness is a dynamic state that fluctuates frequently. Being emotionally well is typically defined as possessing the ability to feel and express human emotions such as happiness, sadness, and anger. It means having the ability to love and be loved and achieving a sense of fulfillment in life. Emotional wellness encompasses optimism, self-esteem, self-acceptance, and the ability to share feelings. The following are a few tips for emotional wellness:

- Respond to situations, not react.
- Show empathy.
- Cultivate an optimistic attitude.
- Practice stress management techniques.
- Never get angry.

Conclusion

When one is physically strong, he will not get tired and will be able to move to different places. When one is mentally strong, he will be able to think and come up with different ideas. When one is spiritually strong, he will behave more ethically and with responsibility. When one is socially strong, he will be able to build a big and strong network. When one is ethically strong, he will be able to get along with people easily. Thus, for a comprehensive growth and development of personality, consistent physical, mental, spiritual, social, and emotional growth is very much necessary.

4.2

Kaizen

Kai   Zen

変善

Change   Good

Introduction

"Kaizen" is translated as 'kai' means 'good' and 'zen' means 'change', so it means 'change for the better'. This principle is most frequently used in the business world to describe a process for eliminating waste and increasing efficiency. However, it can be applied to our daily life. The concept is valuable for people who want to strive for continuous improvement on a more personal level.

Kaizen encourages people to take baby steps towards larger goals and aiming for a 1% improvement each day. Just as drops of water can erode stone by persistence, small actions will add up to become big changes in life.

Steps

The following are steps on how to implement this philosophy in our daily life:

1. Ask Simple Questions

When we have a goal, sometimes we are stuck on how we can achieve it. It is because we see that goal from afar, and not realizing that it takes several steps to make it true. Now, change that mindset. Break down a goal and ask questions like, 'What is the first thing I can do to make it?' or 'Can I spend a few minutes a day doing it?' Stick to the concept that nothing comes easy, it needs goodwill, perseverance, and consistency to make our goal comes true.

2. Create a Process

Come up with an actionable process for a specific activity that is organized and repeatable. Examine whether the process is efficient by asking if the process saves time and if it accomplished our desired result. If not, we need to change it and should not stick in one fixed thing and keep innovating because our world is constantly changing.

3. Prioritize Actions

Now we know the steps to achieve our goals and have the processes set and ready. Now it's time to decide on the order in which we will pursue them. We need to start with the action that will be easiest to implement and go from there. We need to easy on ourselves, but we need to stay disciplined and consistently keep doing the actions.

4. Make Most of the Time

If we look at our daily schedule, it seems impossible to make time for ourselves to stop and do something to reach your goal. However, we will need time to take those small steps. Every night before we go to sleep, we need to review our schedule for the next day and be realistic. Find a slot when we can take some time to do something to reach our dream, and discipline ourselves. We should not delay and fell that you can do it on some other day.

5. Visualize

We need to visualize our goal and how we can definitely achieve it in the small steps that we make. Every day, we need to picture this in our minds, especially when we start the day in the morning. We should not think about the challenges and hardships we may face in achieving it. We need to see our goal as a fun process that makes us stronger and better every day.

6. Keep Track of the Progress

The concept of kaizen is not a sudden, big change, but small changes that you consistently make daily. We can write down what we do towards our goal each day. Keeping track of our progress will also allow us to make adjustments as needed. Kaizen is an ongoing process, so we will need to keep planning, acting, and adjusting as we go forward.

7. Eliminate Waste and Excess

In our way to achieve our goal, we may find things that are unnecessary and time-consuming. Once in awhile, we need to stop and evaluate how much value each activity adds to our life. If, for example, going to a particular course seems too tiring and ineffective to us, we may want to consider learning it online that is more efficient for us.

Conclusion

These simple ways to practice kaizen should help us to achieve our goals and improve ourselves. It may take a long time to achieve our desired result, but it will be worth the wait. With kaizen practice, we can make our goal comes true while not being so hard on yourself–making the progress more achievable and enjoyable.

4.3

Jack of All, Master of One

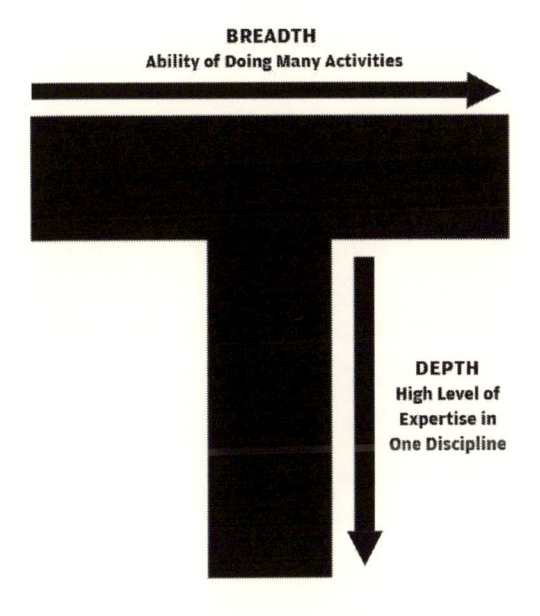

BREADTH — Ability of Doing Many Activities

DEPTH — High Level of Expertise in One Discipline

Introduction

The famous figure of speech, 'Jack of All Trades, Master of None', refers to the type of people who can do many things but fail to become expert in one thing. The phrase was originated in the form of just 'Jack of All Trades' by Robert Greene in 1592 to dismiss William Shakespeare, who was an actor turned into a scriptwriter. It was used randomly as a form of praise by the 17th century until the term 'master of none' was attached to it.

However, in the last few years, the phrase has taken a new form. The new figure of speech is 'Jack of All Trades, Master of One'. The old one was used in a negative reference but the new one is used in a positive reference. The word 'Trade' is used in the phrase, it is most probably used in the field of business and industry, but it can also be applied to various aspects of life as well.

Concept

It is always better to be 'Jack of All Trades and Master of One'. This type of concept is called T-Shaped Personality. The concept is explained below with the help of a diagram.

'Breath' refers to a person's ability to do many activities. As and when a person goes through various phases of his life, he tends to learn many things, intentionally and unintentionally. 'Depth' refers to a person's ability to do one activity with a high level of expertise. Doing many things is easy, but it is the depth that truly makes a person great. A person can gain depth in a particular field or skill, only with consistent effort.

Pros of Being 'Master of One'

The following are the pros:

1. Excellence

A person who is a 'master of one' activity, will be able to do his work in the most effective and efficient manner. The result that he delivers would be very high in quality and close to perfection. Due to which the desired result could be achieved in a short span of time.

2. High Productivity

Since a master of one activity is an expert of what he does, it ensures that he will be extremely productive in his work and his work is most likely to be flawless. So, being a master of one skill can not only increase productivity, but it also increases its accuracy and efficiency.

3. Resourced are Saved

If a 'jack of all activities' kind of person is recruited, he will need a certain level of expertise to ensure quality, then a lot of resources will be required to train him to become efficient. But, if a person who is an expert in the field is employed, he will need no training, thus, saving a lot of resources.

Conclusion

Great people are generally a master of one and have a decent knowledge of various disciplines as well. Today, the fast-moving, competitive and technological world, many activities are performed by machines with the help of Artificial Intelligence, and if people have to sustain themselves, then they will have to be experts in a particular filed, which are difficult to find. People with certain expertise will all be in demand and they will be respected in the market. This kind of mastery can only be achieved by consistently working hard and spending a decent amount of time in the respective discipline.

4.4

Conscious Competence

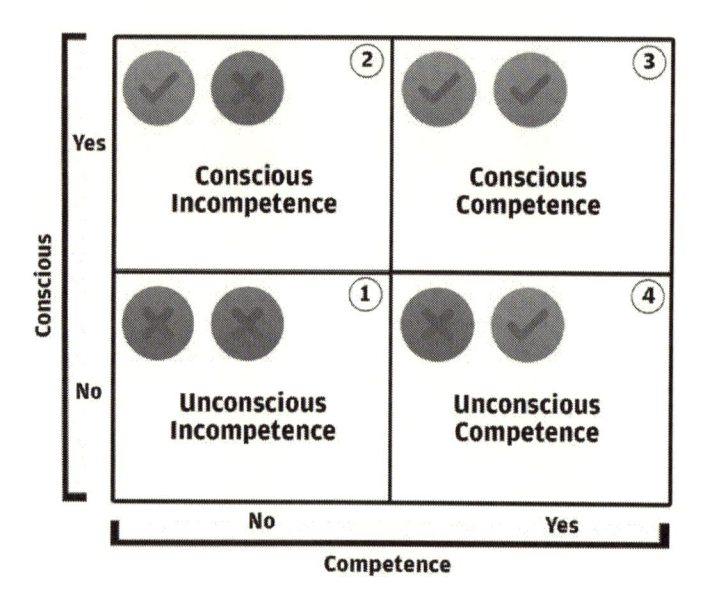

Introduction

Learning a new skill is not a one-day activity, it is a process and process will take time. To understand the process of learning, let us take two significant parameters, competence and conscious.

1. Unconscious Incompetence

This is a stage where we don't know that we don't know. For example, a newborn child does not know that there is a device called a keyboard that exists (unconscious), nor he can type using a keyboard (incompetence).

2. Consciously Incompetent

This is the stage where we know about the activity but we are not competent to use it. For example, when the child becomes two years old, he sees his father using the keyboard to type a document (consciously), but he is not capable of typing even a single word (incompetence).

3. Consciously Competent

This is the stage where we know about the activities and we are able to execute it. For example, when a child grows up and goes to tying classes for two months, he gets to know about the science of typing (consciously) and becomes capable to type something in a decent manner (competent).

4. Unconsciously Competent

This is a stage where we become an expert in the activity and we are able to execute it. For example, when a child is typing he doesn't have to think (unconsciously), and he is capable of enough to type a document in an effective manner (competent). At this stage, we don't need a high level of concentration and thinking, because the behavior pattern has become automatic. He just has to sit in front of the keyboard and he will be able to type without seeing the keys. For example, if we ask a person where is alphabet 'V' in the keyboard, he will not be able to tell, but when he sits in front of the keyboard, his finger will automatically go to 'V', when he has to type 'V'
. This is 'Unconsciously Competent'.

Conclusion

One should identify his interest and consistently invest more and more time in the activity. This would help us to reach the stage of 'Unconsciously Competent'. If one has to achieve excellence in any activity then one has to work consistently towards it. Inspiration will get us started, motivation will keep us on track and consistency is what makes it automatic.

4.5

Conscious Competence

Like any other plant, the growth of the Chinese Bamboo Tree requires nurturing, water, fertile soil, and sunshine, every single day. In the first year, we see no visible signs of activity. In the second year, again there is no growth in the soil. The third-year and the fourth year, we still see nothing. The only thing we know is that the result is supposed to come in four years. But then what happens in the fifth year is just awesome. We see a small bamboo sprig, then the next day an even bigger one and in 6 weeks it has grown up to 90 feet (27 meters).

Had the farmer stopped watering the plant at any point during those four years, it would have died. Had the farmer dug up his little seed every year to see if it was growing, he would have stunted the Chinese Bamboo Tree's growth. If we can be consistent and have patient, every drop of water makes a difference.

Did the Bamboo Tree grow in the last 6 weeks, or was it growing for the last 4 years? It's obvious that the bamboo was growing underground the whole time without visible evidence, but it was growing. Had the tree not developed a strong unseen foundation, it could not have sustained its life as it grew. It was developing the solid root system necessary to support the height and weight of the bamboo stalk for a lifetime.

The Chinese Bamboo Tree is a perfect parable to our own experience with personal growth and change, whether we are working on ourselves or coaching others. It is never easy as it is slow to show any kind of progress. Growth can be expected with consistency and patience. It is also frustrating and unrewarding at times, but it will be rewarding in the long run. People, who consistently and patiently toil towards worthwhile dreams and goals, building strong character while overcoming adversity and challenges, develop a strong internal foundation to handle any kind of situation, and excel in their activity, which leads them to success in the long run.

Some dreams may take months or even years to accomplish. If we start working on our goals and dreams today but don't see immediate results, will we continue tomorrow? How much consistency, faith, and patience will that require? Successful people don't stop, they move forward, even if they don't see immediate results. They know that if they put in the effort, doing the right things every day, then results will eventually come. We need to know that every step we take makes an impact. We may not see the change right away, but if we work consistently towards it, we will definitely able to achieve the impossible.

4.6

Life Long Learner

Introduction

Different methods have been adopted to measure the development of nations. At one point in time, it was literacy, then it was number of people completed their matric, one point of time it was the number of people completed their graduation, and so on. Today, the scale which is used to measure the development of a nation is the 'Lifelong Learning Index'. A person may have attained any degree, but if he does not strive towards lifelong learning, then he would be outdated very soon.

When we are kids, we ask questions like, why is the sky blue, why do birds fly. But as we get older, the curiosity goes away. If we are happy with the knowledge we have, then we are dying slowly. When a person is a lifelong learner, it helps him to be self-confident, stay mentally healthy, fight boredom, creates a curious and hungry mind, keeps him up to date on current issues; keeps the person motivated, helps in growing his network, keeps the person involved as active contributors to society, helps the person to contribute positively for a longer duration and helps in adapting to change.

As the transition from an industrial society to a knowledge-based society, the source of national competitiveness is also changing. In this context, lifelong learning has become a new competitive strategy for countries.

A conceptual framework developed by UNESCO's International Commission on Education for the twenty-first century. The framework identifies 4 important pillars of lifelong learning:

1. Learning to Know – Formal Education System
2. Learning to Do – Vocational Learning
3. Learning to Live Together – Learning for Social Cohesion
4. Learning to Be – Learning as Personal Growth

Lifelong Learning is understood as a continual process of personal and social development and is understood to reflect not only the benefits that employability and a competitive economy offer but also the individual and social benefits of health, happiness, and citizen empowerment. According to this perspective, the objectives of learning need to reflect a holistic understanding of the individual and combine a variety of knowledge, skills, values, and attitudes. From this perspective, the aim of learning is to enhance the qualities of self-esteem, resilience, and a positive attitude towards learning, to develop critical thinking and the ability to learn new things. Thus, lifelong learning can only be attained through consistency.

4.7

10,000 Hours

Malcolm Gladwell is the author of the book 'Outliers: The Story of Success'. Millions of copies of the book have already been sold. The book was also in the list of bestsellers by 'The New York Times' and others. Throughout his book, Gladwell repeatedly mentions the '10,000 Hour Rule', claiming that the key to achieving world-class expertise in any skill is, to a large extent, a matter of practicing the correct way.

Bill Gates, who is one of the richest persons in the world, met the 10,000 Hour Rule when he gained access to a high school computer in 1968 at the age of 13, and spent 10,000 hours programming on it. Gladwell explains that reaching the 10,000 Hour Rule, which he considers the key to success in any field, is simply a matter of practicing a specific task that can be accomplished.

The principle holds that 10,000 Hours of 'consistent practice' is needed to become world-class in any field. Consistence practice means practicing in a way that pushes your skillset as much as possible. If one wants to complete 10,000 hours in a particular field, then he will have to spend around 14 hours every day for 2 years or 10 hours every day for 3 years or 7 hours every day for 4 years or 6 hours for 5 years. But, generally, people take 10 years to reach the 10,000 Hour Rule.

Consistency would yield great results in the long run. For example, if we read 20 verses of the Qur'an every day with commentary, then we can finish one commentary every year. If we read 10 pages of a book every day, at the end of one year we would have read 12 books. If we write one page every day, we would end up writing 1 book at the end of every year. If we convey the message of Islam to 1 person every day, we would end up conveying the message of Islam to more than 350 people in one year. If we teach 20 verses of the Qur'an every week, to a group of people, then we would teach them the entire Qur'an in 6 years. If you learn one new skill every year, you would end up with 5 new skills after five years.

There is no point being 'Jack of All – Master of None', but what would be effective is if a person becomes 'Jack of All – Master of One', and this can only happen through consistent behavior. The question is do we want to achieve excellence in what we are doing or we are just happy and satisfied with achieving average.

To achieve greatness in any area, to become truly great in any area, we have to put in 10,000 hours of practice. No one is born a success, we must work or way there. Most people aren't prepared to put in 10,000 seconds, let alone 10,000 hours. If we are a true winner, if we are really consistent and committed, 10,000 hours is nothing. 10,000 hours is a walk in the park. 10,000 hours is fun, because it's not about how long it takes, it's about whom we become, how skilled we become.

V

Why and How?

5.1
Brain and Consistency

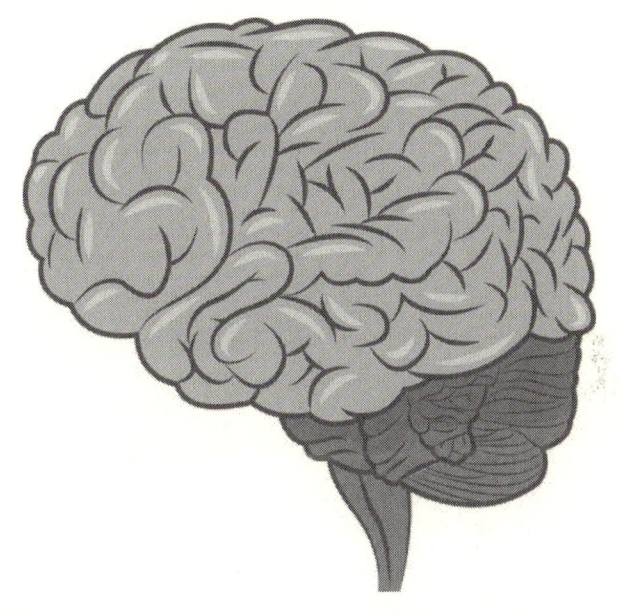

Introduction

Mastering any physical skill takes consistent practice. The practice is the repetition of an action with a goal of improvement and it helps us perform with more ease, speed, and confidence.

What does consistent practice in our brains to make us better at things?

Our brains have two kinds of neural tissues, grey matter, and white matter. The grey matter processes information in the brain, directing signals and sensory stimuli to nerve cells. The white matter is mostly made up of mostly fatty tissue and never vipers. In order for our bodies to move, information needs to travel from the brain's grey matter to down the spinal cord through a chain of nerve fibers called 'axon' to our muscles.

How does consistent practice affect the inner working of our brain?
The axon that exists in the white matter is wrapped with a fatty substance called 'myelin'. It is this myelin covering which seems to change through practice. Myelin is similar to insulin on electrical cables; it prevents energy loss from electrical signals that the brain uses, moving them more efficiently, along with within a row pathway.

Some recent studies in mice suggest that the repetition of a physical motion increase the layers of myelin that insulates the axons. The higher the number of layers, the greater will be the insulation around the axon chains, forming a superhighway for information connecting our brain and muscles. So, many athletics and performers attribute their success to muscle memory. Muscles themselves do not have memory; rather it is the myelination of neural pathways that give these athletes and performers their edge with faster and more efficient neural pathways.

There are many theories that attempt to quantify the number of hours, days, months, and even years of practice that it takes to master a skill. Mastery is not simply about the number of hours of practice, it's also the quality and effectiveness of that practice. Effective practice is consistent, intently focused, and targets content or weaknesses that lie at the edge of one's current ability.

How can we get most out of our practice time?
1. Focus on the task at hand
Minimize potential distractions by turning off social media, mobile, television, laptop, etc. In one study researchers observed that 260

students studying, on average those students were able to stay on task for only 6 minutes at a time. Facebook was particularly the root of most distractions. We need to start out slowly or in slow motion. Coordination is built with repetitions whether correct or incorrect. If we gradually increase the speed of the quality repetitions, we have a better chance of doing them correctly.

2. Frequent Repetitions with allotted Breaks

Studies have shown that many top athletics and performers spend 50 to 60 hours per week on their related activity. Many divide their time used for effective practice into multiple daily practice sessions of limited duration.

3. Practice in Brain in Detail

It is a bit surprising, but a number of studies suggest that once a physical motion has been established, it can be reinforced just by imagining it. In one study, 144 basketball players were divided into 2 groups. Group 'A' physically practiced on handed free throws, while group 'B' only mentally practiced them. When they were tested at the end of the two-week experiment, the intermediate and experienced players in both groups and improved with nearly the same amount.

Conclusion

As scientists get closer to raveling the secrets of our brain, our understanding of effective consistent practice will only improve. In the meantime, effective consistent practice is the best way we have of pushing our individual limits achieving new heights and maximizing our potential.

5.2

Secret of Achieving Mastery

Introduction

Deliberate consistent practice is a mindful and a highly structured form of learning by doing. It is a process of continuous experimentation to first achieve mastery and eventually full atomicity of a particular skill. A 2014 study published in 'Psychological Science' argues that deliberate consistent practice can increase our performance by 26% in games, 21% in music, and 18% in sports. The following are certain tips on how to do it effectively:

1. Define Success and Drill Deliberately

Define all the elements we need to practice to become successful, and then drill each element deliberately, one after another.

2. Reflect and Plan

Plan the practice routine in a notebook. After each session, we need to write down what we have discovered, what worked, and what did not. The idea is to get a clear sense of how a particular session improved our skills and then experiment with new and better ways to achieve our goals.

3. Go Slow

To build a good foundation of muscle memory, we need to practice slow and correctly. If we move too fast we miss learning and internalizing the wrong skills which can bring terrible consequences. To achieve mastery, our brain needs time to develop. Thus, we need to start slow and gradually increase the speed, until we give all we have got.

4. Limit Sessions to Focus

Deliberate practice is hard mental work. We need to limit the sessions to a reasonable duration which will help us to stay focused. This can be as less as 15 minutes if we are young and can go up to 60 minutes if we are old. To keep the attention high, it is recommended to indulge in different activities with breaks.

5. Maximise Practice Time

We need to spend as till time as possible time in activities which do not contribute to our goal. By this, we would save a lot of time and instead use that time for our practice and maximize our practice time.

6. Track Small Improvements

The smaller the data points we measure, the faster we see progress. The more we feel motivated to continue.

7. Emulate Practice and Not Performance

The top performed we see is the result of endless hard work behind the screen. If we want to become like someone we should not see how they perform but we should see how they practice.

8. Repetition

A famous proverb states, 'Practice makes a Man Perfect'. In the 1990s a team of German Psychologists revealed that it takes 10,000 hours of deliberate practice to become a professional.

9. Routine

To reach mastery we need to practice consistently, mostly on a daily basis. We can start by practicing for 15 minutes every day and then gradually increase the time of practice.

10. Have a Guide

The job of the guide is to show us our true potential and guide us in the right direction. It can be your parents, a teacher, a friend, a relative, or even someone whom we find online.

Conclusion

The deliberate consistent practice works for both our mind and muscles. Great people indulge in deliberate consistent practice works for both our mind and muscles. Great people indulge in deliberately practice consistently by taking other people's anger, suspicion, and mistrust and giving them patience, tolerance, and compassion in return.

ABOUT THE AUTHOR

Dr. Syed Kazim is an author, proficient speaker, trainer, psychometric analyst, and a voracious reader. He has completed his MBA, and Ph.D., in the field of Management. He is an author of several books in the field of business, management and personality development. He has written number of articles on Islam, political, economic and social issues, which are published in various print and online magazines, such as, Radiance Viewsweekly, The Companion, Young Muslim Digest, Chatra Vimash (Hindi), Sanmarga Weekly (Kannada), Rafeeq-e-Manzil (Urdu), Youth Ki Awaaz, etc. He has developed various training modules on Leadership, Life Skills and Personality Development. He takes a keen interest in the field of Human Resources Management, Marketing, Psychology, and Counselling. He utilizes his time in reading, writing, and research. He is currently working as an Associate Professor at a Business School in Bengaluru and heads the Entrepreneurship Cell at his institute.

Made in the USA
Columbia, SC
17 September 2022